DEVELOPMENT FIRST

STRATEGIES FOR SELF-DEVELOPMENT

David B. Peterson, Ph.D. & Mary Dee Hicks, Ph.D.

A companion volume to
LEADER AS COACH:
STRATEGIES FOR COACHING AND DEVELOPING OTHERS

Personnel Decisions International
2000 Plaza VII Tower
45 South Seventh Street
Minneapolis, Minnesota 55402-1608

Thanks to the following people for their help in producing this book:

*Don Birkeland, Tom Eckstein, Susan Gebelein, Karis Rieke Gust,
Dave Heine, Lowell Hellervik, Barb Iacarella, Susan James,
Susan Mundale, Bob Muschewske, Steven Snyder, Karen Stellon,
Takao Suzuki, Seymour Uranowitz, Jim Warner*

Special thanks to our clients, who helped us craft and test these ideas.

Design: The Kuester Group
Illustrator: Paul Zwolak
Photographer: Scott Sayers Photography
Editorial Services: Mundale Communications, Gwen Stucker
Printing: Litho, Incorporated
Copyright 1995 by Personnel Decisions International

Printed in the United States of America.

ISBN 0-938529-13-7

CONTENTS

FOCUS ON PRIORITIES: IDENTIFY
YOUR CRITICAL ISSUES
AND GOALS.

IMPLEMENT SOMETHING EVERY
DAY: STRETCH YOUR
COMFORT ZONE.

REFLECT ON WHAT HAPPENS:
EXTRACT MAXIMUM LEARNING
FROM YOUR EXPERIENCES.

SEEK FEEDBACK AND SUPPORT:
LEARN FROM OTHERS' IDEAS
AND PERSPECTIVES.

TRANSFER LEARNING INTO NEXT
STEPS: ADAPT AND PLAN FOR
CONTINUED LEARNING.

DEVELOPMENT IS NOT OPTIONAL

Because of the rapid changes taking place in today's workplace, we discern two new critical success factors:

1. *Individuals* must learn and apply new skills quickly.
2. *Leaders* must help others learn new skills and change their behavior.

No matter what your job is, you feel pressures to work faster, smarter, and better.

To stay competitive, you have to develop new capabilities to do more with less, reduce cycle time, improve processes, stay abreast of technology, launch programs, and devise new market strategies. And if you don't continually improve these capabilities, you will fall behind. Development is not optional.

While the case for development is urgent and compelling, you need not be overwhelmed by it. You can learn how to develop your capabilities efficiently and effectively. DEVELOPMENT FIRST is a proven, practical way to integrate development with your responsibilities and goals so you can do your job better, now and in the future.

Experience is a powerful teacher, but experience alone does not ensure development. Consistent, reliable learning comes only with an understanding of *how* you learn. DEVELOPMENT FIRST shows you how to learn and provides some of the most powerful development tools available.

This approach is not complex, but it does require serious commitment. Development requires time, but much less than you may expect. The secret is to invest a few moments every day – in the right situations – to maximize learning. To leverage your time, we will help you take a realistic look at what you want to achieve, show you what you can do to get there, and demonstrate how to overcome the barriers in your path.

Experience alone won't ensure development.

Finally, we believe that development is serious business, but it isn't deadly serious. We hope that this guide helps you chart a productive *and* enjoyable course to your development.

Best wishes!

David B. Peterson & Mary Dee Hicks

THE APPROPRIATE FRAME OF MIND...

Thomas Edison, founder of General Electric, is famous for inventing things that revolutionized our world – the light bulb, alkaline batteries, the phonograph.

His quote (at right) sets the stage for the development mindset: a willingness to experiment and persistently try new things, even if you make mistakes. Even though he failed 5,000 times on the light bulb alone, no one thinks of Edison as a failure. In fact, he is one of the greatest success stories in American science and business.

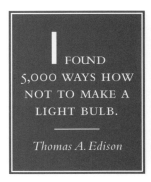

I FOUND 5,000 WAYS HOW NOT TO MAKE A LIGHT BULB.

Thomas A. Edison

Imagine a conversation between Edison and his boss (if he had one...):

Boss: "Well, Tom, it's time you and I had a serious conversation about your performance. How many years have you been at this now? After 3,000 failures in two years, you have nothing to show for it. I think we better reassign you..."

Tom: "No, just give me another 2,000 chances. I'm getting closer. I know I can do it."

Like Edison, your persistence and diligence in development will pay off. Also like Edison, in the long run your successes will matter more than your failures. Mistakes are a problem only if you repeat them, don't learn from them, or lack care in what you try in the first place. If you are smart about your developmental experiments, they won't blow up on you, but they will teach you something even if you fail.

CHANGE
BEFORE YOU
HAVE TO.

———

Jack Welch

Jack Welch, CEO of General Electric during one of the most revolutionary organizational changes in contemporary business, anticipated the need for change and did something about it – before the need was apparent to others.

His approach to business transformation is just as relevant to personal transformation: Look ahead. Change now, while you have the time. Don't wait for a crisis.

When your world is stable and you are succeeding, nothing around you will compel you to change. You need to find incentives, and you probably don't have to look far. If your competitors are raising the bar or your organizational climate, customers, or career options are changing, you need to change to keep pace.

Change before you have to.

WHO IS RESPONSIBLE FOR YOUR DEVELOPMENT?

Traditionally, bosses are responsible for developing their staff. In this approach, bosses deliver performance evaluations once a year, often including a list of things to improve. Now, many organizations are shifting responsibility to employees, making them accountable for upgrading their skills and keeping themselves employable.

Each of these approaches alone misses the mark. Your development requires a *partnership* between you and your organization.

Development requires a partnership.

- *You* need to commit to relevant development goals and then invest time and effort.
- *Your organization* needs to set clear expectations for you and provide appropriate resources, support, and incentives to help you succeed.

In a competitive and changing world, mutual commitment to development is the only way to keep pace and thrive, both for you and your organization.

Your development partners. Help can come from many sources — a coach, boss, colleague, or mentor. Even people outside your organization are prospects. Your partners may be any people who can help you learn and who care about you and your development.

Actively search for development partners who:
• Have access to resources you could use.
• Know other people who could help you.
• Are good at something you struggle with.
• Can help keep you on track.
• Can provide support and encouragement.

Think about everyone as a potential source for coaching.

Think about everyone you meet as a potential source of advice, counsel, or feedback. No one person will fill all of your needs, so keep the list broad.

Since many issues require management support, such as access to resources and permission to engage in various activities, you should also enlist your manager as a development partner.

At the end of each DEVELOPMENT FIRST step, you will find pointers on the best ways partners can help you. Throughout the process, think of the kind of help you would like from others and how you are going to get it.

Your coach. To get the most out of your development process, you need a coach who understands what you are trying to accomplish and how the learning process works. Your coach should be someone you trust who is willing to be candid with you. The coach's level or role in the organization is less important than the ability to observe you, give straight feedback, and help you think about new ways to do things.

So identify a coach and make sure they are familiar with the concepts in this book. At the end of each step, you will find tips specifically addressed to your coach.

DEVELOPMENT FIRST

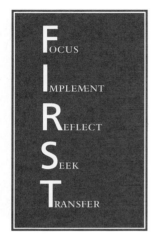

Five simple steps can drive your development and establish a cycle of continuous learning.

1. **Focus** on priorities: Identify your critical issues and goals.

2. **Implement** something every day: Stretch your comfort zone.

3. **Reflect** on what happens: Extract maximum learning from your experiences.

4. **Seek** feedback and support: Learn from others' ideas and perspectives.

5. **Transfer** learning into next steps: Adapt and plan for continued learning.

After you consolidate your experiences in the final step, cycle back to the beginning to focus on your next priority for learning. Soon, this will become a natural, automatic process that transforms you into a virtual learning machine.

These steps alternate between an inward and an outward focus.

• **Focus inward.** Steps 1, 3, and 5 focus inward to help you determine what you want to learn and ensure that your experience becomes conscious, deliberate learning. These steps teach you the ongoing process of "learning to learn."

• **Focus outward.** Steps 2 and 4 require action and interaction with others. The experiential side of learning helps you test and enhance new skills and competencies.

The rest of this book will walk you through each step and help you devise an approach that works for your personal style while avoiding the pitfalls that block learning and development.

As you read through the DEVELOPMENT FIRST steps, you will find lots of advice and suggestions. Don't try to do everything at once. Focus your effort on the one or two points that seem most useful to you right now. Put them into action and get as much as you can out of them.

Don't try to do everything at once.

Since development is ongoing, you will have plenty of time to work on other suggestions the next time you cycle through the process.

FOCUS

---

1. FOCUS ON PRIORITIES: IDENTIFY YOUR CRITICAL ISSUES AND GOALS.

DEVELOPMENT FIRST

Step 1
FOCUS ON PRIORITIES: IDENTIFY YOUR CRITICAL ISSUES AND GOALS

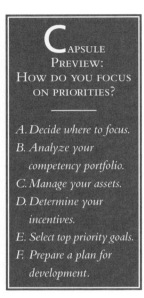

CAPSULE
PREVIEW:
HOW DO YOU FOCUS
ON PRIORITIES?

A. *Decide where to focus.*
B. *Analyze your competency portfolio.*
C. *Manage your assets.*
D. *Determine your incentives.*
E. *Select top priority goals.*
F. *Prepare a plan for development.*

Ambitions that are too high set you up for failure, but those that are too low result in changes that make little difference. If you lack clarity of purpose and a realistic gauge of what you can accomplish, you may aim for the wrong targets, squander your resources, or be so ambitious that any prize eludes capture. To ensure that you change in ways that matter, you must craft your options into a workable, meaningful development direction.

The practical realities of your work life also demand that you focus. There is already so much you must do as part of your job with precious little time or resources to go around. Unless you focus on what is *most* important for your development, you will do what is easiest or most obvious. Or, worse yet, you may do nothing at all.

Our advice to you: *Focus*. Consistent focus on your priorities will prevent you from feeling overwhelmed. Genuine progress on your two or three most important goals is far more rewarding than negligible progress on a dozen less critical fronts.

DECIDE WHERE TO FOCUS

As a starting point, envision two or three of the most successful people you know and ask yourself: What made them successful?
• Drive and ambition?
• Intelligence and foresight?
• Good fortune and circumstance?
• Persistence and resilience?
• The right skills?

Most people succeed because of their strengths; they are bright, motivated, and talented in some way. But let's look at the other side of the coin. Do these successful people have any weaknesses?

Of course they do. No one is even close to perfect. So what makes the difference between those who excel and those who don't? People succeed on the basis of their strengths, as long as their weaknesses don't get in the way.

People succeed on the basis of their strengths.

Likewise, your goal is not to achieve perfection. Rather, it is:
• To leverage and build on your strengths.
• To make sure your weaknesses don't get in your way.

To achieve these goals, you must first *know* your strengths and weaknesses. Personal insight is the starting point.

Analyze your competency portfolio

To reach your full potential you need a good handle on where you stand now. So, heed the dictum: Know thyself.

You might assume that you are already an expert on yourself. After all, who else has spent as much time with you in so many situations across the span of your life? Yet, no matter how well you know yourself or how insightful you are, it is difficult to be so disciplined and discerning that you remain *objective* in your self-assessment.

To analyze your competency portfolio, look at your "Gaps":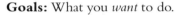

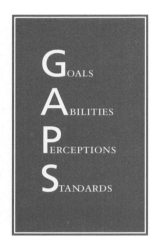

Goals: What you *want* to do.
• Goals are the internal motives and values that drive your behavior.
• To understand your goals, think about what is important to you at work and in the rest of your life, as well as why those things are important.

Abilities: What you *can* do.
• Your abilities include your knowledge and skills and the different ways you can apply them.
• To evaluate your abilities, look at where you have been successful and what you have done that has contributed to your success. Then look objectively at your skills in situations where you have not been as successful and determine what skills would have led to success.
• You may also consider a professional assessment of your personality, skills, and potential.

Perceptions: How *others* see you.

- Others' observations, and how they interpret those observations, can differ from your perceptions and intentions. A full picture of yourself needs to include the view through other lenses.
- You can learn about others' perceptions by asking for feedback and using feedback surveys that ask several of your coworkers for their perceptions of your skills. A 360-degree survey collects feedback from multiple sources, including peers, superiors, and direct reports.

A full picture of yourself includes the view through other lenses.

Standards: What others *expect* from you.

- Standards are the criteria you must meet in order to succeed.
- Standards vary depending on the organization, the environment, the cultural setting, the position, and even your own track record.
- You can ask people about their expectations for you. You can also scrutinize examples of others' success and failure in your setting.

Gather data from as many sources as you can – yourself, colleagues, friends, and professionals. Keep track of what you learn. Look for the common themes and patterns. Try to make sense of any contradictions or discrepancies you find.

A GAPS analysis provides insight into your competency portfolio. To keep your perspective current, reevaluate your portfolio every few years or after any major learning experience.

MANAGE YOUR ASSETS

If people are an organization's most important assets, then each person's development must be carefully managed for maximum short-term returns as well as for future growth.

Leverage your strengths. People succeed because of what they do well. To focus on your strengths, think how you would answer these questions in a job interview:
- Why should we hire you?
- What are you good at?
- What special qualities and abilities would you bring to our organization?
- What things have people praised you for?

Your answers to these questions summarize what makes you a valuable employee. Plan how you will use your unique qualifications to stay on the cutting edge and make sure you are not only valuable but *in*valuable.

Balance your portfolio. Focus on the gaps between your current capabilities and the requirements of your job. Look for answers to these questions:
- To do all aspects of my job well, I need to be better at _____.
- If I were better at _____, I would excel relative to my peers.
- If I improved _____, I would fix an ongoing problem.
- In my performance reviews and other feedback, I have been told more than once that I could improve _____.

Invest in the future. Look for gaps between your current capabilities and what you need in the future. Talk to your boss and other leaders in your organization about how the organization's plans could affect your opportunities. Find out what skills will be at a premium in the future. Review the organization's strategic plans and read about industry trends to determine what capabilities will be most valuable. You can also map out your most likely and preferred future roles. Talk with people in those roles to understand which skills distinguish those who succeed from those who don't.

Then fill in the blanks to these questions:
- In the future, my organization will need people who are good at _____.
- In my next likely roles, I will need to be good at _____.
- As I dream about what I want to do some day, the main things I need to learn are _____.

Determine your incentives

Your personal commitment depends on clear incentives. Look for payoffs for each item on your Leverage, Balance, and Invest lists. Those items that are important to your current and future success *and* for which you have strong incentives make the final cut and become the focus of your development plan.

Find personal reasons to develop. Review the items that are important to your success and determine your incentives for pursuing each. To help you get started, here are some common incentives:

• I want to contribute more and to have a bigger impact.
• I need these skills to be more effective in my job.
• I get personal satisfaction from expanding my horizons.
• With these skills I will feel more confident and better about myself.
• I want to stay current on technical developments.
• If I were more skilled, my stress level would go down.
• I want new skills so I'm more versatile and ready for future roles.
• Many of these skills are useful in my personal life.

Find your organization's reasons for your development. Because development is a partnership, both you and your organization must benefit from your efforts. To ensure organizational relevance, find items that:
- Fill an important organizational need.
- Deepen organizational expertise in an area that is critical to its ongoing success.
- Give your organization more skills it could use in different capacities.
- Help your organization to change and take advantage of new opportunities more effectively.
- Promote your organization's strategic priorities.
- Enhance competitive advantage.
- Improve customer service.
- Keep your organization on the cutting edge.

Maximize payback. You will ignite the greatest energy and claim the greatest rewards when you capture both personal and organizational incentives in your plans.
- Select the items for which you have identified strong personal *and* organizational incentives.
- For these items, conduct a return-on-investment analysis. Categorize them into three groups: easy, moderate, or difficult to achieve. The highest payback comes where cost and effort are low relative to the payback. For example, an easy development objective that has a moderate payback may well be worth your effort, while a difficult one with moderate payback may not.

Select top priority goals

Now that you have inventoried your competencies, anticipated your paybacks, and identified your incentives, you need to commit to one or two top priority development goals.

Keep the list focused. If you choose too many goals, your efforts will be diffused. You won't see sufficient progress on any of them. But if you select goals that are important to you and your organization, you should have ample opportunity to work on them, find sufficient support, and see the kind of progress that will sustain your development efforts. Your goals should be specific enough to translate easily into action, yet not so narrow that you will have few opportunities to work on them.

Stay the course. Expect your goals to evolve over time. The goal you select today may look somewhat different from the same goal a year from now. Don't let shifting opportunities or the lure of an entirely different goal, distract you from your mission. Resolve now to stick with your goal until you can reap rewards from your efforts. Since you can anticipate that you will continue to work on new goals in the future, discipline yourself to address only one or two now.

Prepare a plan for development

Prepare a plan for development like you would for any other important project or objective. Use your experience writing business or project plans to prepare your personal "plan for development." Many of the same elements are required – goals, time frames, action steps. Find a format that makes sense to you so you will actually use it to overcome obstacles and stay focused on your development.

Here are some questions to help you put your plan into action.

- What are the two or three most important *development goals* and objectives for you to work on?
- What is the personal and organizational *rationale* that will keep you motivated to achieve each objective?
- What are the *new behaviors* that you plan to implement?
- What situations, people, or events will *trigger daily action* and signal that right now is the time to put your new behaviors into action?
- How will you *reflect* on your learning experience and consolidate what you've learned each day? How will you take stock at major milestones to reevaluate your goals and priorities?
- How will you *seek information* to measure your progress? How can you get information and feedback on an ongoing basis as well as at major milestones?
- What other *resources and opportunities* do you need in order to learn and apply your new behaviors (e.g., mentors, advocates, training, books, and support)?

Spend more time on development than on development planning.

Watch for roadblocks. Development isn't easy. Even with clear focus and the best intentions, your development plans could be doomed unless you anticipate obstacles and head them off at the pass. Here are a few common barriers:

- I'm too busy.
- I'm afraid I'll fail.
- I don't know where to start.
- I don't have the resources.
- I don't have enough support.

Identify your own barriers.

To keep yourself on track, inventory the barriers that may keep you from your development priorities.

- Write down your highest payback item.
- Outline the most likely reasons you won't act on it. Don't just limit yourself to the reasons we've listed. It is important to identify your own barriers. Be honest with yourself.
- Inventory the barriers for your next two highest priority items as well.

For now, just list the barriers you anticipate. In each of the following steps, you will find practical suggestions to help you overcome the most common barriers.

Don't wait for perfect clarity. Uncertainty is a fact of life. Sometimes, in spite of the uncertainty, you just have to pick something and run with it.

Even after careful thought and analysis of your development goals, you might find that your development focus is still somewhat blurred. You might not know precisely what you are shooting for. As one manager described:

"In the past, my job was very straightforward, like *speed skating*. I had a clear goal and clear standards of success. My performance was measured by a cesium clock, which is precise to the 10,000th of a second. I knew exactly how well I was doing, how I stacked up to the competition, and what I had to do to get better.

"Now, my job is more similar to *figure skating*. It's a complex task, with elements of creativity and personal judgment. Standards, direction, and actions are less clear. To do well, I have to understand what the judges want. The problem is, they all want different things: some of the judges prefer power and dramatic jumps; others prefer elegance and grace. And I know that the Norwegian judge will always evaluate me favorably and that the Swedish judge won't."

When you look to others for direction, you will hear conflicting recommendations. Don't stop asking, but remember that ultimately what you choose has to be your own. Think about who *you* want to become and how *you* want to live your life.

As this manager learned, you will have to take risks and make tough decisions to be successful. There are very few right answers any more, and most of them will change.

There are very few right answers.

Involve others

Tips for getting help from others.
- Find people who can help you clarify your current strengths and weaknesses.
- Ask for guidelines for selecting one or two development priorities.
- Solicit ideas and reactions on your development priorities.
- Determine others' expectations for your current and future performance.
- Get input on future work options and what skills each requires.
- Discuss possible incentives for your development.

Tips for your coach.
- Provide specific, candid feedback on both strengths and weaknesses.
- Set realistic expectations for the amount of development support that is available.
- Clarify existing barriers to development.
- Describe the payoffs that are likely to result from development.
- Encourage commitment to one or two focused goals.
- Communicate current and future organizational needs and how they relate to development priorities.
- Share ideas on the competencies that are most important for the future.

Action steps

It is easy to just keep reading and never put ideas into practice. So take
a moment to crystallize what you have learned about focusing on
priorities and decide what you will do differently because of what
you have learned.

Learning is a personal experience that depends on your goals and
who you are as an individual. No one else can dictate what is going to
be most valuable for you. But two questions can help you take action
on Step 1.

What have you learned so far?
• Without looking back at the chapter, what are the most significant
  lessons or points that stand out in your mind?
• Review the chapter and note additional ideas that apply to
  your development.

What are you going to do differently?
• Select one or two of the most useful insights that you just listed.
• Next, think about how you can act on each idea within the next
  24 hours, as well as within the next week.
• It helps to have a clear plan of attack to help you put your
  insights into play. Consider where, when, and with whom you
  will take action.

Here are additional questions to consider before you move on to the
next step in your development.
• How will you get feedback on how people perceive you?
• How will you learn about what it takes to be successful in future roles?
• What are your two or three most critical development priorities today?
  Five years from now?
• What kind of plan will you use to keep your focus on development?
• How will you make sure you prepare and follow your plan?
• How can your coach and other development partners help you
  at this point?

IMPLEMENT

---

2. IMPLEMENT SOMETHING EVERY DAY: STRETCH YOUR COMFORT ZONE.

DEVELOPMENT FIRST

Step 2

IMPLEMENT SOMETHING EVERY DAY: STRETCH YOUR COMFORT ZONE

CAPSULE
PREVIEW:
HOW DO YOU
IMPLEMENT SOME-
THING EVERY DAY?

A. *Spend five minutes a*
   day on development.
B. *Be opportunistic.*
C. *Be proactive.*
D. *Take intelligent risks.*
E. *Face your barriers*
   head-on.

The book *In Search of Excellence*, by Peters and Waterman, identified "a bias for action" as a prime characteristic of excellent organizations. There is a striking parallel in personal development. All the planning and knowledge in the world will not enhance your performance if you don't *do* something. In fact, most knowledge is useless until you act on it.

You will certainly want to learn new ideas. But lack of knowledge is rarely the most significant barrier to development; lack of action often is.

SPEND FIVE MINUTES A DAY ON DEVELOPMENT

Development is similar to an exercise program. Twenty minutes of aerobic exercise every other day will quickly get you into shape. That's about five hours a month. If you spent those five hours one Saturday a month in a concentrated burst of strenuous activity, you wouldn't get fit. In fact, your body would probably suffer more than benefit. Similarly, one intensive training program each year, with no practice, reflection, or support back on the job will rarely yield true developmental fitness.

The easiest *and* most effective way to develop is to chip away at it in small, bite-sized pieces. Even five minutes a day, used wisely, can make a tremendous difference.

Development *activity* has to become a regular part of your daily discipline. Since you are already busy, you need to guarantee that your time is well spent. To avoid squandering your daily dose of development, focus on situations with high-voltage change potential:

Focus on situations with high-voltage change potential.

High stakes, where you are directly responsible for the outcome, where success or failure will make a difference and be noticed.

Novelty, where you are forced to think and act in new ways because you can't draw on what has worked in the past.

Challenge, where you must do more with less or do it faster and better than you ever have before.

Interaction, where you must work with or through people, particularly when you are working with someone more skilled than you are, on a new team or with a larger group than you have before.

The next time you find yourself in a high-stakes situation that is challenging, novel, and interactive, remind yourself how much you are about to learn!

BE OPPORTUNISTIC

Find opportunities to learn in what you are already doing.

Since time is in short supply, link your goals with something you are already doing. You probably face a dozen opportunities each day to perform more effectively in meetings, conversations, or problem solving. Take a moment each morning to examine the development opportunities that are right in front of you. Then push your comfort zone!

Leverage a strength.

- Try a new angle. *Example*: You can leverage solid writing skills by drafting or editing work for your boss or someone else as part of a joint project.
- Add one new element. *Example*: Build on your strong strategic ability by paying attention to strategic issues in every decision, even very tactical ones.

Balance your portfolio.

- Face the challenge in front of you. *Example*: Coach a difficult employee yourself instead of passing the task to someone else.
- Address unresolved problems. *Example*: Work on your planning and organizing skills by spearheading a process improvement project.
- Find a need and fill it. *Example*: Strengthen your leadership skills by championing a new idea or initiative.

Invest in your future.

- Do old things in new ways. Take a new approach to something just for the sake of cultivating a sense of exploration. *Example*: Try a new way to run department meetings to see how you can make them more effective.

- Look for openings. Scan your environment for events in which you can learn something beyond the scope of your job. *Example*: Volunteer to make a presentation on behalf of your boss or your department. Ask to attend meetings where topics that are new to you will be discussed.

- Walk a mile in someone's shoes. Step back from your work to determine how the issues look from different perspectives. *Example*: Consider the perspective of a customer, someone from a different department or function, or someone who is two levels higher than you in your organization. Ask yourself what you would do if you were in their place; then ask them what they would do if they were you.

BE PROACTIVE

Don't wait for great opportunities to come knocking on your door.
The best prizes come to those who seek them.

Reframe current opportunities. Think of a part of your job that
you handle easily. A good indicator is thinking to yourself, "I could do
this in my sleep." How can you add a new challenge to the routine tasks
of preparing reports, planning and running meetings, or solving
technical problems?
• Can you make it strategic?
• Can you teach others to do it?
• Can you streamline it for others?
• Can you get it done in half the time?
• Can you make it ten times more effective?
• Can you use it to accomplish another part of your job?
• Can you revolutionize it?

Seek new opportunities.
• Ask for new assignments and responsibilities relevant to your priorities.
• Expose yourself to a network of people who are doing what you
  want to learn.
• Get involved in a cross-functional or cross-department activity.

Save time. So far, these suggestions may sound like they require a lot of
your time. The truth is, sometimes they do. So look for opportunities to
save time by trading work with others or redefining your role.
• Swap work. Give someone your assignment in exchange for one
  of theirs.
• Volunteer for a task that would typically go to someone else. To save
  time, do this instead of volunteering for the same old assignment.
• Coach someone else to do familiar tasks instead of doing them yourself.

TAKE INTELLIGENT RISKS

- What if I fail?
- What if it doesn't work?
- What if I look foolish?

Danger lurks behind every developmental foray. Discomfort with risk has stalled many otherwise successful people. You can't let inevitable short-term fears overshadow your development incentives.

Fear of failure is one of the chief reasons people don't try new things. So recast your notions about failure and just get out there and do it. Easier said than done? Here are some tips to make it easier:

Redefine success.
- Separate what you are *learning* from how you are *performing*. Ask "What have I just learned?" instead of "How did I just do?"
- Lower your standards temporarily. Anytime you try something new, you won't meet the standards for things you already do well. You also won't meet your ultimate standards for the new skill. Remind yourself, "This is something new, I don't have to be perfect yet. As long as I'm still learning, I only have to do it well enough to get by."
- Ask people to cut you slack. If you are concerned about criticism, ask others for their patience as you experiment with something new. Set the expectation that you won't be good yet.

Separate learning from performance.

Redefine failure. The author of a recent article on competitive downhill skiing claims that "the more you crash, the more you learn." Quoting a World Cup downhill champion, "In the starting gate, you've gotta lay it out there. You have to make a choice. If you stay inside your comfort zone, you can make it. If you go outside, you fall. If you go on the edge, you win. Racing is a process of learning where that edge lies."[2]

Learning comes at the boundary between being stretched to the limit and going over the edge. You will never find this limit unless you are willing both to fail and to keep trying.

Experiment. Think of yourself as a scientist and of your development activities as experiments. Your immediate goal is not to achieve a specific result but rather to learn what works and what doesn't. Systematically test different approaches, learn from what happens, and formulate the next experiment. Each round brings you closer to your goal.

Take intelligent risks. You must be willing to venture into the unknown. If you know how you will fare before you start, you won't learn much. Intelligent risks are those with both a reasonable chance for success and a reasonable measure of doubt. Move ahead in small steps that push you into the unknown without taking you over the edge.

Intelligent risk taking is what Thomas Edison was doing – systematically trying new things that had a reasonable, but not certain, chance of success. He wasn't foolhardy, but he persisted until he found what worked.

> ONE DOESN'T DISCOVER NEW LANDS WITHOUT CONSENTING TO LOSE SIGHT OF THE SHORE FOR A VERY LONG TIME.
>
> *André Gide*

FACE YOUR BARRIERS

Action is the essence of development, so you must knock down any barriers that prevent you from taking action. Since you have now tried some new behaviors, you have probably encountered some snags. Bring your barriers into the light of day so you can address them honestly. Here are some common barriers and a few thoughts about what you can do.

1. PROCRASTINATION, INERTIA, AND LACK OF TIME.

- I'll work on this next week.
- There isn't enough time.
- I'm too busy.
- There are too many things going on.
- If I don't stay on top of all these fires, I won't even have a job!

What can you do?

- Make development routine. Set aside a regular time, such as the first meeting or project of the day. Devote five minutes and make a small investment every day rather than looking for a big chunk of time.
- Commit to others. Set due dates and make a public commitment to create urgency and pressure on yourself. Share and regularly review your goals with your coach or development partner.
- Make development a *job* priority. Include it as part of your annual objectives and hold yourself accountable in terms of performance requirements.
- Make it easy. Set specific, reasonable objectives that don't require a huge up-front commitment. Set smaller goals and don't expect dramatic changes now.
- Create reminders. Write your goal where you will see it every day.
- Revisit your incentives. Reassess your personal and organizational reasons for development. Make sure the payoff is salient.

Set smaller goals and don't expect dramatic changes now.

2. FEAR OF FAILURE.

- I'll cause problems for other people if I bomb.
- I'll look foolish if this doesn't go well.
- Everyone will lose confidence in me if I don't pull this off.
- I'm afraid the rest of my job will suffer.
- I can't afford to make a mistake.

What can you do?

- Determine the real risks. Talk to others to assess the likelihood of failure. Place odds on the realistic negative outcomes. If the odds are high, readjust your plan to lower the risk. Ignore fears that are not well founded.
- Face the fear. The best way to eliminate fear is to do what you are afraid of and then realize that nothing terrible happens. Unrealistic fears persist if they are untested.
- Create a safe haven. Start low profile and low risk. Find a safe place to test your wings.
- Read Tom Peters' *Thriving on Chaos* or *The Tom Peters Seminar*[3] in which he talks about the importance of risk taking.

Find a safe place to test your wings.

3. Feeling stuck.

- I don't know where to begin.
- I'm not sure what else I'm supposed to do.

What can you do?

- Start with a low hurdle. You may be trying too hard to find the perfect starting point. Begin with what you already know and look for simple things to try. Then raise the hurdles to a more challenging level.
- Seek suggestions. If you truly have no idea what to do, solicit ideas from others, read a book on the topic, or take a training course. Ask people in similar situations what options they see for themselves.
- Get clarity. If you are still stuck, you may need to go back to Step 1 and make sure that you have focused on high priority needs.

Involve others

Tips for getting help from others.
- Ask others to help you find opportunities to try new behaviors.
- As you try new things, negotiate realistic expectations about how much you will accomplish and what standards you need to meet while you are learning.
- Discuss how others have dealt with the problems you are facing.
- Swap tasks or responsibilities with coworkers so that you can work on something new.
- Ask for feedback as you try new things.

Tips for your coach.
- Create safe opportunities for experimenting with new behaviors.
- Point out unnoticed development opportunities.
- Encourage people to engage in development activities they may avoid.
- Identify how existing strengths can be deployed.
- Provide a fresh perspective on how to approach an old situation.
- Rotate assignments among your team.
- Help arrange for support from others.
- Communicate realistic performance standards; don't expect competence from a novice.
- Praise development efforts, not just results.
- Assign responsibilities that stretch current competencies.
- Be a model for development by openly pursuing learning and taking risks.
- Remove organizational barriers to development activities.
- Allocate resources for development, including money, time, and consultation.

ACTION STEPS

Once again, it is time to crystallize what you have learned and translate that into action.

What have you learned so far?
• Without looking back at the chapter, what are the most significant lessons or points that stand out in your mind?
• Review the chapter and note additional ideas that apply to your development.

What are you going to do differently?
• Select one or two of the most useful insights that you just listed.
• Next, think about how you can act on each idea within the next 24 hours, as well as within the next week.
• Finally, develop a clear plan of attack that considers where, when, and with whom you will take action.

Here are additional questions to consider before you move on to the next step in your development.
• Where are the best places to try new things in your current role?
• How can you find new situations and opportunities for trying new things?
• How will you remind yourself to do something every day?
• How will you respond when you try something new and things don't go as planned?
• How can your coach and other development partners help you at this point?

REFLECT

---

3. REFLECT ON WHAT HAPPENS: EXTRACT MAXIMUM LEARNING FROM YOUR EXPERIENCES.

DEVELOPMENT FIRST

Step 3

REFLECT ON WHAT HAPPENS: EXTRACT MAXIMUM LEARNING FROM YOUR EXPERIENCES

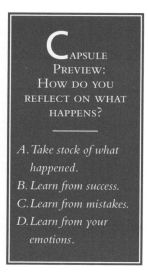

CAPSULE
PREVIEW:
HOW DO YOU
REFLECT ON WHAT
HAPPENS?

———

A. Take stock of what
   happened.
B. Learn from success.
C. Learn from mistakes.
D. Learn from your
   emotions.

Development requires action. And reflection on what you have done is the foundation for continued action.

Your reflection should be purposeful, not unstructured time lost in thought. The goals of reflection are to:
• Solidify your insights and make sure you remember the lessons you just learned.
• Identify the themes and patterns in what you do. Only over time can you see your progress, habits, and limits. When you understand these patterns, you can accumulate learning and systematically chart your next steps. Without this understanding, instead of ten years of experience, you may end up with one year of experience ten times.
• Question and challenge your assumptions to make sure you learn the right lessons and remain open to new learning.

Take stock of what happened

Take time to reflect on your development experience. Ask yourself questions that will help you identify what you have learned and how to use it in the future.

What should you ask?

The short view: What can I learn from my developmental experiences today?
• What worked and why?
• What didn't work and why?
• What could I have done differently?
• What assumptions do I need to challenge or change?
• How did I conquer my barriers and how did they get in the way?

The long view: What are the larger patterns and trends over time?
• How does my current skill level compare with what it was when I started my development?
• How does my current skill level compare with my goal?
• What progress can I feel good about?
• Which challenges keep arising?

The context: How are my actions related to factors in the environment?
• What people or situations do I handle best?
• What are the people or situations that are a particular challenge?
• What are the common elements among those people or situations?
• What are the barriers inside me or in the situation that limit my effectiveness?

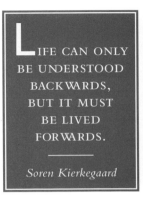

LIFE CAN ONLY BE UNDERSTOOD BACKWARDS, BUT IT MUST BE LIVED FORWARDS.

Soren Kierkegaard

When should you reflect?

Daily doses: If you are doing something for your development every day, you are creating opportunities for reflection every day. Don't let the lessons escape because you didn't bother to capture them. Find the times that work best for you:

- A personal debrief of the day on the commute home from work.
- A five-minute review as you plan the next day.
- One or two minutes immediately following any new action.

Don't let the lessons escape because you didn't bother to capture them.

Periodic reviews: Consolidate your lessons over a span of time. Take ten minutes every week or a half hour every month. Cycles like weeks, months, or even the seasons provide a natural rhythm for review.

Major events: Reflect whenever something significant happens. You solve a crisis, you complete a big assignment, or you pass a major milestone on a project. Allocate time in proportion to the significance of the event and the likelihood that you will face similar situations in the future.

Midpoints: Take stock at the halfway point in large projects. You have some experience behind you and still have opportunities to make a difference if you change your approach.

How should you keep track?

Keep a notebook that will serve as your learning record. A profoundly valuable development tool, a learning record helps you keep perspective, remember your lessons, and demonstrate your progress.

- Keep it brief. If it's long and detailed, you are less likely to keep it up.
- Make it personally meaningful. This is your record and it doesn't have to follow someone else's formula.
- Have fun with it. Don't make it cumbersome.
- Track the most important lessons. For example, you might keep a running list of the ten most important tips that you need to remember or a list of insights about what skills you will need in the future.

LEARN FROM SUCCESS

What better opportunity to learn what works than success? Yet rarely do people give success sufficient scrutiny. Success can blind you with glory or lull you because the challenge is past. In either case, you forego the inspection that reveals what worked and why.

It's OK – even important – to celebrate success. Go ahead and pop the cork. But also take a few minutes to imprint the success pattern in your brain.

Ingrain success in your brain.

Be honest with yourself. Determine exactly what you did to succeed.
• How much of this success was due to my actions?
• What did I do particularly well?
• What did I do that was more effective than what I have done before?
• How did I overcome the barriers to doing this?
• What could have gone wrong that I managed to avoid?

Transfer the learning. Leverage your lessons into other situations.
• What is my next opportunity to try this?
• Are there different situations where I could apply what I have learned?
• What could I do differently that would make this easier next time?
• How can I improve my performance next time?

Find the hidden lesson. Stay open and alert to unexpected learning. Assume that everything you do is a learning opportunity, but that the lesson may not be the one that you want or intend to learn. Cultivate your curiosity to find the free development gift that is hidden inside your daily experiences.

Find the free development gift that is hidden inside your daily experiences.

LEARN FROM MISTAKES

Playwright Oscar Wilde, commenting on a poor audience response to one of his plays, claimed, "The play was a success but the audience was a failure."

Like Wilde, you won't learn much if blame prevents you from looking at yourself when things go wrong. You also won't learn much if you ignore or conceal mistakes. On the other hand, you could try to understand what happened and learn from it. Start by figuring out what went wrong.

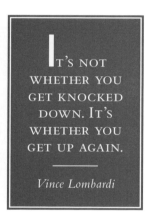

IT'S NOT WHETHER YOU GET KNOCKED DOWN. IT'S WHETHER YOU GET UP AGAIN.

Vince Lombardi

Dust yourself off. No one is perfect. No one wins all the time. Constant learners are resilient. They know that when they push the edge, they are bound to fall. And they don't hesitate to get up and keep playing.

Look at the situation. Some efforts will fail due to factors outside your control. A systems view can help you determine what is realistically in your control and what isn't.
• What factors were outside my control? Be objective so you don't avoid responsibility where it truly applies.
• How can I anticipate them or work around them?
• How can I influence these factors so they don't get in the way?

Own your share. Assume that there are enough things under your control that changing your behavior could clearly produce better results.
• Did I prepare and practice enough?
• Did I draw on the resources and people who could help?
• Did I set realistic goals and expectations?
• What do I need to learn before I try this again?
• Have I had a similar problem before?

LEARN FROM YOUR EMOTIONS

When you start to examine yourself, you may experience frustration, surprise, satisfaction, relief, apprehension, guilt, and anxiety. This is natural.

Listen to yourself. It's common to say, "no pain, no gain," but "naught without thought" is closer to the truth. When you are happy or contented, think about what caused your success and how you can achieve it again. When you are angry, frustrated, or embarrassed, identify the triggers. Then figure out what you can do differently the next time.

Don't run from pain. One problem with reflection is that it doesn't always feel good. But paying attention to your feelings now can help you prevent frustration in the future. Just like physical pain, negative emotions draw your attention to something that isn't the way it should be. Use your emotional pain to:
• Mobilize action. Discomfort can be a motivator for change.
• Draw your attention to something you may be ignoring. Don't let emotions prevent you from examining the situation openly and objectively.
• Identify areas of future growth. If the pain isn't related to a current priority for your development, make a note so you can consider it next time you set goals.

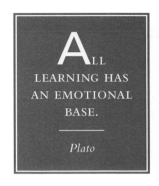

ALL
LEARNING HAS
AN EMOTIONAL
BASE.

Plato

COPE WITH BARRIERS

Each step in DEVELOPMENT FIRST presents its own challenges. Once again, you need to honestly appraise what gets in the way of reflection. Here are some common barriers.

1. NO IMMEDIATE RESULTS.
• I'm not getting anything out of this.
• This contemplation is a waste of time.
• I'm not really learning anything I don't already know.

What can you do?
• Reset your expectations. You won't necessarily learn something every day. Insight builds, drop by drop, until you eventually accumulate a pool filled with useful information.
• Focus on a simpler process. Ask one or two good questions that zero in on the primary things you want to learn.

2. SOCIAL PRESSURES.
• I'm changing, but I'm getting pressure from others not to rock the boat.
• If I change, they have to change.
• If I get better, it might make my colleagues look bad.

What can you do?
• Reassess the payback to you. The balance of pros and cons may shift.
• Enlist others in supporting your change. Ask for their help and assistance in a way that doesn't fault their own behavior.
• Explain that you need to change and then help others move along with you.

3. BACKSLIDING.

- I keep slipping when I take my eye off the ball.
- My old habits come back when I'm under pressure.
- I've changed, but it doesn't work as well as I thought it would.

What can you do?

- Recast this problem as progress. Actually, these insights are not barriers to reflection because they are its productive fruit. You wouldn't see these trends if you hadn't been making some progress! You are beginning to see how the learning process works for you and you have identified a new problem that requires a new set of actions.
- Record as precisely as possible what happens when you slip. Look for trends so you can fortify yourself when you anticipate those situations again.
- Recognize that change requires time and practice before it becomes natural. It also proceeds in fits and starts, moving two steps forward, then one step back. Your changes will stabilize and become easy only with persistence and practice.

INVOLVE OTHERS

Tips for getting help from others.
- Reflection is primarily an individual activity. One way to involve others is to encourage them to help you take the time to reflect.
- Another way to involve others is to have them help you think things through so you can figure out what happened and what you can do differently.
- Test your assumptions and conclusions with others to ensure you are on the right track.
- Talk through your frustrations with someone who will just listen.

Tips for your coach.
- Encourage regular time for reflection.
- Make time for regular discussions of what has been learned and how it has been learned.
- Ask questions that force people to think things through for themselves.
- Realize that sometimes all you need to do is listen.
- Provide suggestions on what to do differently.

ACTION STEPS

What have you learned so far?
• Without looking back at the chapter, what are the most significant
  lessons or points that stand out in your mind?
• Review the chapter and note additional ideas that apply
  to your development.

What are you going to do differently?
• Select one or two of the most useful insights that you just listed.
• Next, think about how you can act on each idea within the next
  24 hours, as well as within the next week.
• Finally, develop a clear plan of attack that considers where, when,
  and with whom you will take action.

Here are additional questions to consider before you move on to the
next step in your development.
• How will you build time for reflection into your routine?
• Which barriers will likely keep you from taking time for reflection?
• How will you structure and maintain your learning record?
• How will you determine what caused your successes and failures in
  specific situations?
• What emotional reactions to success and failure can you use to identify
  your learning opportunities?
• How can your coach and other development partners help you at
  this point?

SEEK

---

4. SEEK FEEDBACK AND SUPPORT: LEARN FROM OTHERS' IDEAS AND PERSPECTIVES.

DEVELOPMENT FIRST

Step 4

SEEK FEEDBACK AND SUPPORT: LEARN FROM OTHERS' IDEAS AND PERSPECTIVES

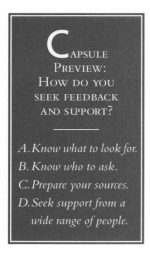

CAPSULE
PREVIEW:
HOW DO YOU
SEEK FEEDBACK
AND SUPPORT?

A. *Know what to look for.*
B. *Know who to ask.*
C. *Prepare your sources.*
D. *Seek support from a*
   wide range of people.

People typically provide feedback because they like what you are doing and want you to continue, or they dislike what you are doing and hope you will stop.

Feedback is important to you for other reasons.
• Feedback tells you if you are on course and how to correct if you veer off.
• Feedback sustains your motivation. You have to work hard to focus, implement, and reflect on your development. You need to know if your efforts make a difference.
• Feedback lets you see yourself as others see you. Your picture of yourself, and consequently your self-assessment and goals as well, are incomplete without it.
• Feedback is central to your development partnership with others.

Feedback is a conversation that provides you with personally relevant information that helps you make informed choices about what to do.

Look at the components of this definition:
- Because feedback is a conversation, it requires give-and-take dialogue. Hit-and-run messages from others ("Here's your performance review. Call me if you have any questions.") don't qualify as feedback.
- Feedback must be personally relevant because you'll ignore information that isn't connected in some way to your goals and concerns.
- Because feedback is information, it is nonjudgmental and nonevaluative.
- Feedback helps you make choices because it is instructive. It not only describes what *is*, it points to what you could do the same or differently in the future.

Feedback is a conversation.

How do you get feedback?

Obviously, you want feedback that is relevant to your development priorities. But think about exactly what kind of information will be helpful and who can provide you with that information.

Know what to ask for.
- If you are just beginning to work on something, you may want fairly broad feedback on what you have done. As you advance, you may seek feedback on more specific details.
- If you are leveraging a strength, general feedback on how well you do will teach you little. You need specific feedback on how well you are deploying that strength and how to enhance it.
- You may want feedback on different elements at different times. For example, if you are working on being a more influential leader, you might look for feedback on how well you involved others and shared leadership in a staff meeting. Yet after a presentation you might want to know if your speech was inspirational and compelling.

Know who to ask.
- Get input from a variety of people. The more perspectives you seek (friend and foe, internal and external, bosses and peers), the more complete your picture. Like illuminating a scene with spotlights from different directions, the shadows disappear.
- Keep the source in mind. Seek feedback from a variety of people, but assess their expertise as well as their opportunity to judge your skills accurately. Think about how seriously you should take their feedback.
- Cultivate key sources. Identify two or three people from whom you can regularly seek feedback. You should trust them enough that you are willing to share your development goals with them. They must trust you enough to tell you honestly how you are doing.
- Be opportunistic. Seek feedback from anyone who has the opportunity to observe you and will be honest with you.

Seek feedback from a variety of people.

Prepare your sources.
- Instruct people so they can give you the kind of feedback you need.
- To get more than "Well, you did just fine," you need to alert your sources to the specific feedback you want. Focus their attention *before* they observe you so they know what to look for.
- Let people know you are serious about wanting feedback. Share your development goals so they understand your purpose.
- If your development needs are extreme or obvious, people are bound to notice. However, if you are building on strengths or fine-tuning a skill, people may have a hard time seeing what you are working on. You'll probably have to ask them to watch for very precise points.

Time it right.
- If someone has watched you in a specific situation, seek feedback while it is fresh. Keep the discussion short and focused on what just happened.
- If you want to know how you have done over a period of time, schedule a brief discussion. Allow your sources some time to think about what they have observed.

Make it easy.

- Focus on your visible behaviors and your sources' reactions. Ask what they saw and how they interpreted your actions.
- Just listen, don't quibble. Ask questions to make sure you understand, but don't argue, debate, explain, disagree, or justify your behavior. Make it as painless as possible for them to give you feedback.
- If you aren't getting helpful feedback, ask specific behavioral questions that can be answered with simple facts or with yes or no: Did I interrupt anyone? Whom did I interrupt the most? Did I ask everyone for input? Whom did I leave out?

Look ahead.

- Ask for advice about what to do differently.
- Thank people. It's not always easy giving feedback. Let them know you appreciate the time they spend helping you. Keep them willing to give you feedback again.
- Finally, put relevant feedback to visible use. If people see that you act on the feedback you receive, they will be more willing to give you constructive, honest feedback in the future.

Put relevant feedback to visible use.

How do you get support?

In addition to feedback, you need others to sustain you in the ongoing hard work it takes to really change. Development is not a private endurance contest. There are many ways others can help:

Encourage you to try new things and keep development as a priority.

Give you freedom to make mistakes. Your boss, at minimum, needs to cut you some slack.

Offer assignments or responsibilities that will require you to try new things.

Provide you with opportunities to see bigger vistas or rub shoulders with the experts. You need access to the people who know what you want to learn. Use the experts in informal mentoring relationships, invite them to critique your work, or get invited to their meetings.

Share moral support so you can express your fears and concerns openly.

Provide financial resources for books, tapes, and other training materials; classes, conferences, seminars, or even a sabbatical assignment. When you ask others for financial support, provide a tight rationale that conveys your goal, what you have already tried, and the expected payoff from the investment.

You will probably need time to focus on development activities. Negotiate some room in your list of obligations to make development a priority. Ask for reduced productivity or results expectations when you are trying something new. This is a tough request to make, but it may be the deciding factor in freeing you to attend to your development.

Many people can give you sage advice and counsel and help you gather new ideas and critically examine your knowledge and assumptions. You might cultivate a relationship with one individual or systematically engage a series of people in exploring ideas. Pick their brains on their areas of expertise and engage them in dialogue about your ideas. Strive to sharpen your thinking and strategies. Set a specific objective for your discussions, such as, "Can you go through last month's P&L with me and explain how you interpret it?" or "I have a few ideas about our market strategy I would like to test out with you."

WHAT'S IN IT FOR THOSE WHO SUPPORT YOU?

Development is a partnership, which suggests benefits for all parties. If you seek support from others, provide something in return. Consider the following ways you might repay their support:

- Take a few minutes to learn about their goals and determine where you might have something to offer to them.
- Express your appreciation. Pick up the tab for lunch or send a brief thank-you note.
- Indicate your willingness to return the favor for their assistance.
- If they would like it, give them some good press. Let others know that they were helpful to you.
- Finally, remember that their time is valuable; don't waste it.

Who can give you support?

You can get help from virtually anyone. Even bad role models and poor advice can give you insights on what you should avoid or do instead. Ask yourself what you can learn from anyone you deal with. In addition to the role of your coach, consider how the following people can assist your learning:

Colleagues, peers, and direct reports. They are great sources of feedback and moral support. They have often faced development challenges that are similar to yours.

Your boss or team leader. Your management has control over resources, opportunities, and rewards. Their success is often tied to yours, so they have a vested interest in maximizing your performance.

Human resources staff. They can often provide objective perspectives and counsel, direction on learning opportunities, and guidance on outside resources.

Role models. Watch what they do and emulate actions that are compatible with your style and goals.

A mentor. Mentors have considerable knowledge and experience, and they are willing to share it. They may not know the process of learning, but they are rich in expertise.

Most mentoring is brief and short-term, so it does not require a formal or extensive commitment. If you think of mentoring as a process, not a person, you are free to consider how a variety of people can play different mentoring roles on different subjects across time.

Look for mentors who:
• Have a successful track record.
• Have the knowledge, skills, or abilities you need.
• Have the time and willingness to talk and listen.
• Have a broad resource network.
• Initiate coaching contacts with others.
• Are respected.
• Will encourage you to take risks.

OVERCOME BARRIERS

1. LACK OF FEEDBACK.
• I don't get enough feedback.
• I don't get the kind of feedback I want.
• My boss won't give me feedback.

What can you do?
• Examine yourself. Make sure that you are not the barrier to feedback. Make it easy for others by asking for the right input and listening to all input without defending or explaining your position.
• Persist. Many people aren't really sure that you want honest feedback. Don't just ask once, then disappear, waiting for them to find you. They'll open up as they become certain of your sincerity.
• Read between the lines. People often try to be nice and may not say exactly what they mean. Piece together the subtle patterns in feedback from different people to find underlying trends, then confirm your understanding with them.
• Ask, don't wait. As with all steps in development, be proactive.
• Try different formats. Not everyone can provide immediate face-to-face feedback. Provide people with options such as a written critique of your work, a short phone conversation after they have had time to consider their opinion, or even anonymous feedback from surveys.

2. Lack of personal support.

- My boss won't help me.
- No one has any time for my development.
- I'll look weak if I admit I want support.

What can you do?

- Expand your network. Don't limit your search for support to the
  traditional roles of your boss and the human resources staff. Direct
  reports, team members, and colleagues often have a strong vested
  interest in your development and will help you as long as they don't
  fear reprisal or other consequences.
- Cultivate relationships that can give you support without
  strings attached.
- Invest in others' development and provide the support they need;
  eventually they may return the favor.
- Show others the organizational payoff and the benefits to them.
  Give them good reason to care about your development.

> Don't limit your search
> for support to the
> traditional roles.

INVOLVE OTHERS

Tips for getting help from others. The essence of this entire chapter is how you can get support from others. Two particular themes to keep in mind are:
• Be proactive in seeking the feedback that you need. Don't wait for it to come to you.
• Ask for support when you get frustrated or discouraged.

Tips for your coach.
• Ask what kind of feedback would be most useful.
• Be generous with feedback – too much is better than too little, too frequent is better than too rare.
• Create opportunities to provide feedback at natural junctures, such as after big events and at the midpoint in an initiative.
• Solidify success with specific praise.
• If you provide negative feedback, suggest what could be done instead.
• Relate your feedback as directly as possible to the person's goals and priorities.
• Be as specific as possible.
• Explain the impact of the person's actions on other people and on results.
• Look for frustration and offer to help remove barriers.
• Provide empathy when you perceive discouragement. Acknowledge that change can be difficult at times.
• Offer help and suggestions for overcoming barriers.
• Summarize your observations over a period of time so you can describe trends in performance.
• You can find a list of other things you can do in the section titled "How do you get support?" on page 65 of this book.

ACTION STEPS

What have you learned so far?
• Without looking back at the chapter, what are the most significant lessons or points that stand out in your mind?
• Review the chapter and note additional ideas that apply to your development.

What are you going to do differently?
• Select one or two of the most useful insights that you just listed.
• Next, think about how you can act on each idea within the next 24 hours, as well as within the next week.
• Finally, develop a clear plan of attack that considers where, when, and with whom you will take action.

Here are additional questions to consider before you move on to the next step in your development.
• How will you identify the people and situations that can provide the most valuable feedback? For each feedback opportunity you identify, ask:
  – Whom will you ask for feedback?
  – When will you ask for feedback?
  – What questions will you ask?
• What else can you do to make sure you get candid feedback on the issues you are most interested in?
• How can you extend your circle of development partners to get broader feedback and support?
• How can your coach and other development partners help you at this point?

TRANSFER

---

5. TRANSFER LEARNING INTO NEXT STEPS: ADAPT AND PLAN FOR CONTINUED LEARNING.

DEVELOPMENT FIRST

Step 5
TRANSFER LEARNING INTO NEXT STEPS: ADAPT AND PLAN FOR CONTINUED LEARNING

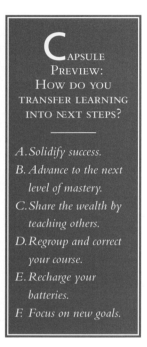

CAPSULE PREVIEW: HOW DO YOU TRANSFER LEARNING INTO NEXT STEPS?

A. *Solidify success.*
B. *Advance to the next level of mastery.*
C. *Share the wealth by teaching others.*
D. *Regroup and correct your course.*
E. *Recharge your batteries.*
F. *Focus on new goals.*

Your development is like a series of chapters in a long but fascinating book. Each new episode builds on the last. Chapter endings — the completion of the major objectives on your development plan — are natural times to take a break and to reflect on where you have been, where you are now, and where you want to go next.

Step 5 helps you use your development experiences from Steps 1 through 4 as a launching pad into the next adventure. You are ready for Step 5 when you accomplish your objectives, when you are stuck, or when you have cycled through the previous four steps several times and need to take stock.

SOLIDIFY SUCCESS

Celebrate accomplishments. If you have accomplished your development goal, take some time to celebrate. Ask people who have partnered with you to share in the celebration. Most people prefer closure on important objectives. Success builds self-confidence and feelings of personal worth. So don't gloss over what you have accomplished.

Keep sharp. Without occasional attention, your skills may start to get dull. Be sure to review your major lessons. Continue to create opportunities to try what you have learned. Then, get feedback to stay on track.

Advance to the Next Level of Mastery

If you have been working on a particularly enjoyable and valuable strength, you may want to go beyond competence to mastery. Masters distinguish themselves by executing even the most difficult tasks with ease. Like great chess masters, they often can:

• See the underlying patterns that others miss.
• Recognize subtle exceptions to the rules.
• Avoid common pitfalls.
• Anticipate longer-term implications.
• Play several moves ahead of the competition.

If you see the payoff for mastery, consider the following strategies for developing a world-class skill.

There is no finish line. **Seek experience in new, complex situations.** Force yourself to face challenges that push your limits.

Spend time with the gurus and experts. Benchmark yourself against the leaders in the field. Get advanced coaching from the very best. Associate with people who are more skilled than you. Watch what they do and continue to push the envelope of your own performance.

Cross-train. Pursue learning in related areas and search for the synergies, connections, and parallel ideas. Take those lessons and translate them into personal action. Read broadly to get new ideas and perspectives.

Through it all:
• Stay curious and continue to ask questions.
• Get comfortable with the fact that you will never have all the answers.
• Look for the learning opportunities in every situation.

SHARE THE WEALTH
BY TEACHING OTHERS

Teaching can double the return on your investment. Not only do other people and your organization benefit when you teach, you also stand to gain. You will:

Deepen your expertise. When you teach others you are challenged to become an expert. Force yourself to articulate and clarify what you know. Allow others to test your assumptions and interpretations. Push yourself to learn more so you stay ahead of your best students.

Grow personally. There are certain lessons that can be learned only by investing in others. When you teach people who are less knowledgeable or skilled you must go at their speed. You can develop an appreciation for others' unique styles and capabilities and for what you can learn from them. Finally, you can forge a deeper understanding of how your knowledge can be applied in a variety of situations with a variety of people.

Learn about learning. As a teacher, you become a student of the learning process. If you watch how others learn, you will discover ideas on how you can learn. Then, apply what you learn from observing and coaching others to your own development. Step outside yourself and give yourself advice.

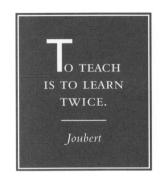

To TEACH IS TO LEARN TWICE.

Joubert

Here are some other thoughts to keep in mind if you are serious about sharing your knowledge with others.

Cast a broad net. Don't limit yourself to coaching the people you supervise. You can help develop anyone, including superiors, customers, and colleagues.

Find an opening. As a coach or mentor, you need to carefully position your help so that others are willing to receive it. Start by learning about their goals and self-perceptions. Ask them how you can be helpful to them. Then, don't force your message. Wait until they are ready to hear your feedback and advice.

Be a role model for development. You can lead others to develop themselves when you seek and listen openly to feedback, share your development goals, and invest time and effort in your own development. Share your learning experiences, especially how you have taken risks and coped with failure.

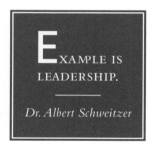

EXAMPLE IS LEADERSHIP.

Dr. Albert Schweitzer

Regroup and correct your course

If you have not been successful so far and you are not sure what to do next, review each of the DEVELOPMENT FIRST steps and try some of the tactics you have not used yet. To increase the chances that your course correction will work, pay attention to the following:

Address your barriers. Review each step in the process with particular attention to the barriers you have encountered. Devise a plan of attack for removing each significant barrier.

Get another perspective. Find someone to evaluate what you have tried and to help you understand why it hasn't worked. Ask people to help you reflect on your progress. Often a fresh perspective will show you a new angle or a novel solution.

Call on a professional. If you are still stumped after genuine attempts to follow the development process, now may be the time to call on a professional in the field of development, either an internal resource or a respected consultant.

RECHARGE YOUR BATTERIES

Development may seem like a lot of work. And it often is! You need to keep momentum and perspective.

Step back. Take a break from time to time. Stop asking for feedback. Spend a month catching up on activities you enjoy and put your career development on hold. Pursue some activities that are purely for your own pleasure.

Be creative. Another way to recharge your batteries is to do some out-of-the-box thinking. Daydream about yourself in exotic future roles that require new capabilities. Talk with people outside your field and learn about their plans and challenges. Read more outside your field to expose yourself to new ways of thinking.

Focus on new goals

You have now completed a full cycle. It is time to take your new knowledge and skills and apply them to your next development priority.

With each cycle the process becomes easier and more natural. You experience rewards from your efforts and risk taking. As others see you grow, they give you new opportunities.

Audit your progress as you conclude one phase in your development and move into the next. Your current circumstances, opportunities, and capabilities should look different from when you started.

Take stock of your gains.
• What can I do now that I could not do before?
• Where can I use these new capabilities?
• Who could benefit from these capabilities?
• How can I let others know that I have these capabilities?

Critique your approach.
• What development tactics and strategies worked best?
• What approaches did not work well?
• What have I learned about how to manage my development?

Assess the context.
• How have my circumstances and opportunities changed?
• How have the players changed?
• How can I use these new circumstances or players as a springboard for further development?
• How might these changes affect my ability to succeed with my development in the future?

You are ready to focus on new goals. You are wiser about how DEVELOPMENT FIRST can work for you. There is always more to learn, but you are in charge. Keep learning!

INVOLVE OTHERS

Tips for getting help from others.
• Discuss your overall level of progress to confirm your perceptions.
• Ask for more challenging opportunities where you can continue to test your new competencies.
• Network to find experts who can help you advance to the next level of skill.
• Ask for ongoing resources and support as you enter the next phase in your development.
• Maintain an ongoing dialogue with people about emerging opportunities for you to learn and apply new skills.

Tips for your coach.
• Expect development to be continuous; sustain your involvement when the original goals are met.
• Run interference when other people, systems, decisions, or policies obstruct development.
• Promote an environment where mistakes are tolerated and development is rewarded.
• Stimulate learning by exposing people to novel ideas.

ACTION STEPS

What have you learned so far?
- Without looking back at the chapter, what are the most significant lessons or points that stand out in your mind?
- Review the chapter and note additional ideas that apply to your development.

What are you going to do differently?
- Select one or two of the most useful insights that you just listed.
- Next, think about how you can act on each idea within the next 24 hours, as well as within the next week.
- Finally, develop a clear plan of attack that considers where, when, and with whom you will take action.

Here are additional questions to consider before you move on to the next step in your development.
- What can you do to get the most additional mileage out of your new skills?
- What would it take to advance to the next level of skill? Is it worth it?
- How can you determine the value of investing your time in coaching others?
- What have you discovered about your best tactics for learning? How can you use them in the future?
- What can you do to stay excited about your ongoing development?
- How can your coach and other development partners help you at this point?

REFERENCES

1 Peters, T. J., & Waterman, R. H., Jr. (1982). *In Search of Excellence.* New York: Harper & Row.

2 Cooper, C. (1994). "Crash Course." *Men's Journal.* February, pp. 83–88.

3 Peters, T. J. (1994). *The Tom Peters Seminar.* New York: Vintage Books. Peters, T. J. (1987). *Thriving on Chaos.* New York: Alfred A. Knopf.

BIOGRAPHIES

Mary Dee Hicks and **David Peterson,** Senior Vice Presidents at Personnel Decisions International, have devoted much of their careers to helping organizations and their people become stronger through the development of individual talents. As psychologists and leadership coaches, they have cultivated practical approaches to development that have been consolidated into workshops, presentations, and publications, including DEVELOPMENT FIRST: *Strategies for Self-Development* and *Leader As Coach: Strategies for Coaching and Developing Others.*